Natalie Fastovski

Thank you for inspiring

the villains in my art

you created all of this
by breaking my heart

short prose, poetry

and weird art

Natalie Fastovski

Thank you for inspiring the villains in my art

you created all of this by breaking my heart

short prose and poetry

Acknowledgements

a special thanks to:

Eda Aydogan
Katharina Stumpf
my editors
my former teachers
and everyone who inspired the villains in my art.

Content

This publication is listed in the German National Library.
Detailed bibliographic data is available via http://dnb.dnb.de.

Published in Germany

© 2021 Natalie Fastovski
Editors: Sarah Zou, Georgia-Taygeti Katakou

Cover and illustrations: Natalie Fastovski

Production and Publisher: BoD – Books on Demand, Norderstedt

ISBN: 9 783753 439921

Don't assume any of this is about me,
but if you read something in this book that makes you
wonder whether I'm writing about you:
I probably am.

SHORT PROSE

thank you

They will always be a part of you, but you will never *be* them.

You will never be them, but they will always be a part of you.

There is a war in your head because there was a war that they caused. You weren't there, but you know. Everyone knows. You are supposed to be someone, to hate someone, to celebrate something because of what they did and what they went through.

Is this you?

You are alive because of them.

"Look at this pose, the way you sit on this chair with your legs crossed and your arm on the table. Look at your posture; you look just like *her*."

The old man points at a black and white picture covered in dust. There is a woman sitting on a chair and staring at something the viewer can't see. Her hair is perfectly braided, she is wearing a long dress and gloves.

You are the villain in someone else's story. Someone, somewhere has looked at this very picture, pointed at it and said, "Those are the people who killed us."

Your world is separated into villains and superheroes, you live in a fairy tale and everyone else does, too. There are only two teams. If you aren't one of *them*, you are the bad guy.

Who are you?

You don't even know everything these people, "your" people, did. How would you know? You weren't there.

You weren't alive. You never told them what to do. You didn't have any influence on what has happened, but you are one of them.

One day, you are just yourself, but you need nothing more than facts to realise that sometimes, you are the one you despise, that you are the one you hate with a passion, just in a later generation and with a different hair colour. They live inside you and the fact that they died when you weren't even alive doesn't change anything. They'll still live on inside you, the wars they caused can't be uncaused, the words they said can't be unsaid.

Who are you if you are not them?

"Do you know why you are sitting in this very chair right now? You should thank them all for it."

But isn't there more? Don't you know yourself better?

"Now look at you. You are just what you were taught: you judge people based on what happens between their bedsheets without knowing them, without knowing their story, without knowing what they feel and without knowing what they went through. You support the values you were taught to support, you hit a dead end when you try to explain your view of the world with logic. 'That's just the way it is' is not an explanation. You raise your kids differently because you say your mother did it wrong, you let them swear, you buy them all the new and fashionable and sparkly little things they so desperately want because your mother didn't. Your mother will always be your mother or at least the one who gave birth to you, but you will always be yourself and the result of the environment that has shaped you."

He doesn't know what to respond or maybe he pretends he didn't hear anything. He just takes the picture of this woman and his bony hands shake as he puts it back into the little box and then onto the shelf that he so regularly examines – sometimes it makes him cry, sometimes it doesn't. Today, it doesn't.

He is probably still tired from the war and everyone knows he needs to rest.

Maybe he will understand one day.

He is alive, because he made it, not because of them.

You will never be them, but they will always be a part of you.

They will always be a part of you, but you will never *be* them – and you should thank yourself for being alive today.

<u>for</u>

Four people who keep up with your immorality their entire lives take you to church twice a year, because you believe in God.

I think I know why you believe in God; you think he's going to save you from yourself, save you from the consequences of being an asshole. Today you said I deserve to die young, tomorrow you'll be in church, praying for those who don't have faith in the divine, praying for atheists like me. The priest is going to talk about sinners, about murderers, about those people who we need to forgive and you will respectfully nod, take your wife's hand and the hand of the person next to you, your kids are far away from you (and I know why, but I bet you don't). You don't know who that guy is, but you take his hand because that's what the priest said you should do and it would be really rude not to; the priest is probably the only person who can give you orders. Well, the priest and sometimes, every now and then, your wife. She would probably look at you in the same way she looks at you when you don't say hello to that co-worker. He smells really bad all the time (just like his son and his brother), no matter if he comes into your restaurant after a very long day of work or if it's the first place he goes in the morning. He does a "really bad job", he's "awfully slow", he's "fat and probably eats all the food when no one is looking". You told your wife he should take a second chair when he sits down during his break, but then again, she gave you that look.

What's worse: an angry wife who doesn't cook your favourite food in the evening or keeping that comment to yourself for the sake of a decent meal? You probably know the answer.

You only open your mouth to scream or to eat the food made by your lovely wife and you don't deserve any of it. Your wife and your three daughters are the only four people who matter to you in this world and you still decide to scream at them as if you will have anyone left if they go.

When you jokingly told me to "have faith" because the cash box didn't open fast enough, I replied, "I'm an atheist!" and you laughed at me, you mocked me for being stupid, just like you always do.

You better pray for me in church, I am obviously so lost.

Poor, poor atheists: they have no morals at all (it was me who kept my thoughts to myself when you audibly wished I would die just because I didn't want to open that window), you are such a good person, unlike me (you always shout, you shout as soon as you enter the room, you shout as soon as you open your mouth, mistakes are something that "don't happen" to you, except when they do, but that's like, haha, "never", right?)

We are all so stupid and you are the only intelligent person in the entire restaurant, no, in the entire world (you almost burnt the noodles, you forgot to empty the dishwasher, you slapped your father in the face when he came in to talk to you because he was "annoying", you dropped out of school because your Spanish wasn't good enough). I don't mean to offend anyone, but if it's not you, it must be your wife who is stupid, because she made the mistake to marry you. But we all make mistakes, don't we?

Yeah, I really think the only time you saw Jesus was when you got too high at Oktoberfest; all of your friends were too high or drunk or both to even notice that you were gone: people screaming and shouting and everything smelling like sweat and alcohol and puke and homo sapiens with bodily functions mashed together in a very horrible place. She saved you and now she is your wife.

You know, when I think about the fact that *you* managed to find a wife, I reconsider my atheism, but the only time you thank God is when you go to church twice a year: Easter and Christmas Eve. But that's enough, isn't it? You pray for the unfaithful and the faithless only because the priest tells you to fold your hands.

Most of all, you pray for yourself twice a year. And every hurried prayer is like the silent demand for a new piece of paper where you can start writing again, start writing just the same crap as you did before.

Correcting mistakes? Hell, no! Just wait until next year and all of your sins will be forgotten and forgiven and will magically fade away.

That's what the church is there for, isn't it? Salvation?

Well.

It must be my lack of faith speaking when I say that you have no morals.

Maybe I should just have *faith* that you'll become a better person. Maybe I should just start praying for you. Maybe we should both pray for each other more, because this is going to change a lot:

We'll both be praying for each other on Sundays and you'll be wishing me death from Monday to Saturday.

inspiring

She met her first boyfriend when she was ten. They went to school together, they did their homework together, they hung out every afternoon long before they were a couple. He brought her flowers every now and then and she knew exactly what it meant. She didn't act on her feelings at first because she knew her mum thought she was "too young to be doing this." It was like a really bad high school movie where straight teenagers pretend there's an insurmountable obstacle just so they can live the drama of their lives and end up together "no matter what".

Now, a few years later, she is telling this story to their kids and trying to teach them a lesson. "Reach your goals", "Never stop fighting", "Don't give up" and whatever else sounds like the wall tattoo of a stereotypical straight, white, cis woman in her thirties. Her kids think she is embarrassing anyway, so they just keep on eating their soup without paying much attention to what she has to tell them.

She works at an office, eight hours a day, sometimes nine, sometimes ten. She leaves the house at seven in her black Polo car and she doesn't ever come back home before five pm.

In the evening, she barely has the energy to cook so she eats leftovers from yesterday and possibly from the day before. She cleans the house; a bit or ironing here, a bit of vacuum-cleaning there to drown out the annoying screams of her children who are constantly bullying each other at this age.

Before she can even realise it, she falls asleep before her husband arrives and wakes up in the morning only to see a messy and empty other half of the bed which, at the moment, is the only proof left of his existence.

When she leaves the house in the morning, she puts on the black coat and rose lipstick. Her brown hair smells of hair spray and the money she makes in the office is often spent on the Chanel perfume she wears on a daily basis. With this smell on her clothes, she goes outside and becomes nothing but a part of a grey, homogeneous mass. Her Chanel N°5 mixes with about two hundred other Chanel N°5 perfumes, she becomes a part of a sea of black coats, brown hair and rose lipsticks. She's just another brown-haired woman in the sea of one hundred and ninety-nine other brown-haired women.

She goes to the hairdresser once a month to get a blowout – time for selfcare, time for herself, time to enjoy the moment and live for no one but herself. After twenty minutes, it's done. She's happy. Her husband doesn't notice any difference – "Is it shorter? Longer?"

And maybe one day, her husband is going to leave her because he has found someone else. Her body has aged, her beauty is gone – she's like a dry flower in dirty water, trying to survive, but inevitably coming closer to death, every day a small piece of her dies and he notices it, things are going to be different, not the way they were before, he'll want someone younger, someone who can take care of him, someone who'll want to live an adventure with him. Was she ever the one he would have needed? The one who would even utter the word "adventure" without saying the word "ridiculous" in the very same sentence?

He won't dare to say any of that out loud. She'll know their marriage is over long before he'll dare to utter the words, but they'll stay together – "for the kids."

Once he'll decide to tell her, he'll probably mumble something about not being good enough, something along the lines of "I don't deserve you anyway". Her children will move out and not call her often enough.

It's very probable that she'll go on a path of self-discovery. Does she even know who she is? She'll find a new hobby like sewing, singing or Zumba. She'll think she's found it: her very true self, the essence of what it means to be her. And she'll think she has learned some kind of lesson. She'll think she has given her life a meaning.

She thinks her story is special. She's going to write a book. She's going to publish it.

She'll think she is inspiring – and so do the five hundred other women with the blue name plate who work in that very same company, so does every woman who, after long consideration, buys Chanel N°5.

the villains

Hello Mrs. Monis,

I want you to think about the title of this. You've always told me to *think*, but now it's your turn.

It's my letter of resignation.

Yes, I'm quitting this job, because you need me more than I need you.

Maybe you should have reconsidered the way you treat your employees when you realised you can't handle all this work alone – but you didn't. The keys to the cupboard with the unpaid invoices are on your desk – most of them are due tomorrow, so let me put this into your words: "you better get started."

Let's reminisce, shall we? Are you ready for a little throwback of the amazing story of our friendship? Buckle your fucking seatbelt. I know exactly you've read this far so let's not pretend like you have a choice.

I met you for the first time when I was about three years old and when my sister's friend introduced me to you, I said to her, "I don't like her."

You were standing next to us. You heard it.

And sometimes, you still talk about how I said I didn't like you when I was three.

Does it give you nightmares? Is that what you think about at night when there is nobody you have to convince that you are the best?

I just wanted to say that I was a very intelligent child.

When I was five, I left a chewing gum on your desk. I repeat: I was *five*.

And sometimes, you still talk about it.

Do you even realise I have never talked about all the crap you have done to hurt me before?

You've done worse things than leave a chewing gum on a fucking desk.

The only reason I've endured this bullshit for so long is the fact that I feel so sorry for my co-worker who will have to deal with you all by herself, without me. But guess what – now she's gone (because you suck) and there's no reason for me to stay any longer.

I don't know if you think you've "won": everything in life seems to be a battle to you, every conversation that you have has a winner and a loser.

What is the price you pay for winning?

Let me just give you a brief overlook of what you've achieved by, well, let's say "just being yourself": there is only one co-worker in the entire history of this company who has worked for you longer than I have and your company has existed for over twenty years now.

It's been really funny watching your reactions to people quitting:

"Is she really too *stupid* to do this work?" (I know she was one of the best and most talented people you had and I also know how much you wish she would come back),

"They all know how to brag, but they are all too *stupid* to work" (You're the one who is bragging, but yeah, sure, let's just ignore the fact that you are anything but perfect.),

"It's so *stupid* of him, this job was his only opportunity" (If he had kept the job, he probably would have killed himself within the next two weeks.)

We're all subconsciously attracted to things that embody us, so maybe "stupid" is your favourite word because it describes you best.

Did I offend you? Am I the villain now?
I didn't forget how you called the people who quit:
"the villains in this fairy tale."

I wonder who you think you are in this wonderful story, written, narrated, directed and produced by no one but yourself.

I, your favourite villain, have found a new job and even if I hadn't, I would quit.

How does that make you feel? Do you think you've won because you hurt me so much I couldn't stand it any longer? Am I the evil dragon that was killed by the brave princess Monis? Did you save this kingdom? Do you think you've won?

If you do, all I can say is: congratulations.

Good luck looking for another employee who is willing to put up with someone like you.

I hope you've found this letter as I attached it: With a chewing gum on the backside of your desk.

<u>in my art</u>

He's in his thirties, he's a businessman, he doesn't have time; no time for anything but meetings, black and silver folders with printed receipts and delayed shipments. Whatever he does in the morning was already due yesterday, he's running (out of time) and never looking back, trying to make up for the work he couldn't catch up with; he thinks about the money, thinks about the kids.

They are already asleep when he comes home: his youngest son is an artist; he paints everything that he can not put into words, he doesn't talk much, because he doesn't have to: whoever doesn't understand his art isn't meant to understand.

When they see each other at the kitchen table and his dad sees the acrylic paint on his fingernails that his son didn't wash off, he starts a conversation about "real work," being an artist isn't going to get him anywhere, painting is a waste of time, no one is going to stand in front of his paintings that are too far away from real life to understand, he does nothing but paint, can't he focus on school, should he take the god damn canvases away from him? What about maths, physics, chemistry? At least some kind of science? A "real man" should be good at these things.

Then they go their separate ways: his father doesn't even know his last chemistry lesson was two years ago and that he's never even had physics in school.

His older son wants to be a nurse. "That's not even a job for men", "Do you know this isn't even going to be enough money to survive?", "Choose a job not with your heart but with your brain if that's what's necessary to survive".

Whenever his dad doesn't tell him any of these things, he's at work and he starts talking about them once he comes back home.

He doesn't do the dishes, because that's what his wife is there for. He doesn't even put them in the dishwasher; women and their kitchens, they have their own rules and their own order, there's no need to intervene. Whenever he comes home, the food is already cooked, it's already on the table, still warm and it smells amazing. His shoes are cleaned for him, his lunch boxes are made for him. That's what women can do best anyway; the last time he tried to cook noodles was more than twenty years ago. He wouldn't know how to do it if he had to. But he doesn't have to.

Not as long as he has his wife, not as long as the food just keeps appearing on the table.

Ten years later, he's carefully reading the instructions of the package. Cooking noodles can't be that hard, right? Boil the water first or put the noodles in first?

In any case, he has to do it by himself now. His wife had left him, his mother had died and there was no one who could possibly teach him.

What an injustice. Didn't he give everything for his family? Didn't he try his absolute best to raise two wonderful, independent sons? Didn't he teach them the important values in life? Didn't he work so hard for the entire family just so they could live in wealth and never had to worry about money?

He tries to call his eldest son, but he's not picking up; he tries to call the younger one, but he's currently launching his 23rd art exhibition in Milan as a full-time artist.

Why doesn't anyone have time? Maybe he could have found the answer in his son's art.

you

I hate it when you play the harp. The lifeless object is not used to being played gently, it almost sounds as if you were punishing the poor instrument; it's supposed to sound beautiful and soft but you only ever play it when you're mad. Your pale, deformed fingers that are nothing but bones hit the helpless instrument that can do nothing but produce a sound in response and I know it would run away if it could and never come back. I'm in the building next to you, the windows are closed, the curtains are closed, yet I can still hear you and I can see your face in front of me even when I close my eyes; you are so focused on collecting all of that rage from the inside and putting it into the triangular piece of wood which seems to be so close to cracking under those bony fingers. Whose soul is more damaged, whose bones are closer to breaking? Your facial expression can't be read, but I know you always feel empty after having been mad. Your eyes are nothing but the window to an eternal path into darkness, a road that leads nowhere but deeper into your own thoughts that can't be understood, not even by yourself. Your feet furiously and mechanically indicate the rhythm that your wrinkled fingers have to follow.

It's way too loud, but every time I think the strings are going to burst, you manage to play even louder, turning the most beautiful melodies into a hymn of madness and destruction.

There is no way to escape your theme song. It represents you well. I can imagine how strangers see you:

they probably perceive you as some kind of floating elf with your white hair, creeping around, not making any sound yourself and only ever using your harp as your lungs, it's the only way for you to get vocal, probably even your only way to breathe. You are trying to express something that no one will probably ever be able to grasp.

Sometimes, you'll rest your head on that harp as if it were to find out whether it was still breathing; to find out whether you had already abused it enough. Sometimes, you'll take an old cloth and slap your instrument with it, trying so hard to clean it from what it had gone through, but your movements are too violent, too quick to clean anything. Sometimes, you'll stare at it with your empty eyes, imagining your next attack, your next crime and yet you know nothing is ever going to be expressive enough. None of the things you do to this instrument are ever going to paint a complete picture of you. None of them are ever going to represent or even partly symbolise who you truly are.

created

Our fingers touch, I don't know what to do – I'm naked in a room full of people.

"This is art.", the artist says and removes his hand from the gentle touch.

Some of them are creeping around; they're ashamed, looking at the floor or standing in the corners, trying to focus on the white walls, but they can't.

I know they want to leave, yet they open their eyes trying so hard to look away. And even those who hide behind their hands, their fingers, their mothers and fathers, they peek.

Some are excited. They touch, they poke, they are running around my cage, examining me.

Life is a zoo and I am a dinosaur. Everyone thinks that I'm dead.

"What does this mean?" the philosopher asks. She looks at my scars. She tries to look into those eyes behind bars but all she manages to do is stare.

"Is she going to die?" the doctor asks. She looks at my bruises, touches my bones and proceeds to look up all my symptoms in her dusty book. Questions and questions and questions and questions. I can't answer.

"Is this about me?" my best friend asks. She cries, I can't speak, she looks at all the photos of times that were better and of grass that was greener; she doesn't recognise me, or maybe she does, but she doesn't recognise herself in me, she doesn't recognise the "me" in the cage, she compares it to the "me" in her photos.

"Is she even real?" the scientist asks, "All these limbs, these broken bones, they're all over the place. It might just be a lie, an illusion. She can not be alive, I can not explain- it has to be an illusion."

I walk into the room and I look at myself in the cage; naked, distorted, broken and numb, but prettier, grumpier - more aesthetic.

Everyone's silent, not believing their eyes and all I can say is, "The artist was right."

all of this

Our summer was wonderful, but now winter is over and I still think about you.

-

Lilies bloom from early summer to fall. The frost during winter can be fatal for lilies. If they freeze to death, they die, never to come back again.

-

I woke up from a sound of breaking glass and found myself in the garden near the bungalow. How long had I slept? I removed the newspaper from my face that was covering my eyes and apparently had helped me fall asleep at least partly hidden from the sunlight and the heat of this summer day.

A girl with long, brown hair was desperately trying to collect pieces of broken glass.

Without thinking, I quickly got up to help her. "Hey, let me help you," I said, collecting the broken pieces.

"Oh." It was a very surprised "oh." Not only did it sound surprised, but also thankful, shy, somewhat like an excuse. "Thank you," she quickly said, looking down. I could tell she was shy and I couldn't help but smile. "I'm... I'm sorry, was that your glass?" the girl asked followed by an awkward attempt to giggle and I knew exactly she was trying to have a conversation with me.

Something about her told me that it would actually break her heart if she had spilled my drink.

"Well, technically, yes. My parents own this place," I replied, "But don't worry. It happens all the time." Before she could say anything or apologise again, I gave her my hand both helping her up and taking the opportunity to introduce myself. "My name's Rose."

For the first time, I got the opportunity to properly look at her face which – I could tell – she liked to cover with her long, brown hair. Her eyes were blue and small freckles decorated her face. I had probably never seen another human being in my life who looked as innocent as her and yet, I knew nothing about her. She nodded, as if she was saying: "I appreciate that you tell me your name," and added, "Lily."

"You haven't been here before, have you?" I asked.

"What do you mean?"

"I mean last year. Or the year before. I haven't seen you around."

At this point, I kind of regretted having started a conversation with her, because her look was saying: "This is none of your business. I don't know you. You don't know me." She was a very cautious human being. Maybe I was wrong and she had never tried to have a conversation with me. Whatever.

"This is the first time I'm here. Probably the last one, too." She paused and then added an explanation, probably not to sound rude, "I love seeing new places all the time."

I couldn't help but ironically smile at myself for the instant stupid fantasy, the thought that maybe there would be a guest one day who would come here every summer, maybe be my companion. It had never happened before. The guests who come regularly are elderly people or couples who like to spend some time alone. Nobody really seems to be interested in the daughter of the people who own this place and I mean – why would they. It was just a stupid thought anyway.

Seeing me smile, she smiled too, followed by a surprising question, "What do you do here?"

"Oh, I just- you know. This and that. I water the flowers," I pointed at the garden I had slept in, "I help my parents out wherever I can and whenever I'm needed."

Lily nodded. "I've seen the garden. 'The garden of Eden'. It's beautiful."

"Well, I will take that as a compliment. I try my best." "What kinds of flowers do you grow?"

"You want me to show you around?" I asked and she nodded.

"Come!"

I jumped in excitement, taking two stairs at a time. If there was one place I knew entirely by heart, it was this – my garden.

"You're too fast," she yelled, "Where are you going? You could have started down here!"

I didn't say anything, just waiting for her as she came up the stairs I had built myself as well. I pointed at a violet flowerbed. "Lilies," I said, "in purple. Like you."

I pointed at her t-shirt.

"I never knew what lilies look like," she admitted.

"You didn't? It's your name!"

"I don't know. They all look the same to me."

I shook my head.

"No. That's not true. They're special."

She raised an eyebrow.

"They... they're *all* special," I added, "Every kind of flower has its own blooming time. Even different kinds of lilies have different blooming times. But all lilies have one thing in common: they attract butterflies. It looks so peaceful when a butterfly lands on a lily. Do butterflies ever land on you?"

Lily didn't seem to know how to react. "I don't- no, I don't think they do."

Was I being too forward? Was I annoying her? My heart dropped as she looked at her watch. "Actually, I should get going."

"Oh, I'm- I'm sorry. I didn't mean to- you know."

"Yeah," she smiled as if it was an apology.

"I'll see you around," she said and disappeared through the flowers.

-

Had I offended her in any way? Was I just being weird? I know I can be like this sometimes. I'm just way too forward. I thought about her as I watered the lilies in the evening, scaring away some of the butterflies.

I hadn't seen her anymore. She seemed to be gone all day long or maybe she was hiding from me. Why would a girl on vacation need to be anywhere at a specific time? She wouldn't. She left because of me. But that's okay. There's not a single reason why it would matter, I told myself as I hid under my blanket as if hiding from somebody and drifted off into sleep.

She was standing in the middle of a huge field of roses. "Rose!" she yelled and started running into the sunset.

"Catch me if you can!"

I was running after her and as I caught her, we both fell into the grass and she picked a rose for me.

"Is it going to die?" she asked me.

"Of course," I answered, "All flowers have to die one day. And that's okay." And she started crying as the entire field was swept away by a tornado, I tried to hold her, but-

I woke up.

-

"Rose!" she yelled.

"Lily!" I almost dropped the hosepipe.

"What?" she asked, "Am I this scary?"

"Maybe."

She was wearing a short black dress and sunglasses. I didn't see her eyes, couldn't tell what she was thinking. Was she hiding from me?

"I mean, no. Of course not," I quickly added.

I couldn't help but ask her where she had been.

"Here and there," she replied. Wishy-washy answer. Not that I was surprised, so I decided to change the subject. "Want to share some strawberries later?"

"I sure do," she said, "You grew them yourself, I bet."

"I did, together with my dad. I had never planted strawberries before. This year was my first time."

I proceeded to water the plants and tried to sound as casual as possible as I asked her, "So, where are you from, actually?"

"I'm from the north of England."

"England, huh. Yeah, I could tell. The Queen's accent sold you."

"The Queen's accent is from the south. I don't speak like that."

"Yeah, you do."

"No! I don't sound that posh."

"To me, you do."

She folded her arms in defence. "Where are you from?"

"Well, technically, here. I was born here, but I only spend my summers and the beginning of spring here. I also have to attend university, you know. It's just a two-hour-drive away from here. Melbourne."

Lily nodded and to my surprise, she kept asking, "So, what do you do when you don't water your plants and when you don't go to university?"

"You really do want to expose me, don't you?" I asked.

"I have no idea what you mean by that." She looked innocent as ever.

"Yeah, you do."

"Okay, maybe I do. Is there anything in this world you *don't* know?"

I stopped the water and put the hosepipe on the floor. "Let's go have some strawberries."

-

I didn't remember how we ended up drinking wine. I didn't remember how we ended up sitting in my Garden of Eden and talking about life. At that moment, all I knew was that I felt good.

I put a strawberry in her mouth when I was sick of her assumptions about me and received a muffled, tipsy giggle.

"I thought you didn't like me," I burst out.

"Nooo," she protested and hugged me, but quickly pulled away.

"Not true," she added.

"Why did your parents give you that name?" Lily asked, "It's as if it was your destiny to grow this garden."

"Well, in a way, it was," I answered and took another sip of our homemade wine, "I mean, my parents owned this place long before I was born. It's a family tradition, you know. But... I never really asked them about my name."

"Hmm, what are roses like?"

"You mean the flowers?"

"The flowers."

"I thought you didn't like it when I- know stuff."

"I never said that."

"Well... there are lots of different species from all around the world, so..."

"Yeah, but what are they *like*"

"Well... roses have thorns."

Lily was quiet for a while.

"The pollen of lilies are nearly impossible to wash away from fabric."

"You looked it up," I said. It wasn't a question.

Suddenly, I felt her head lean against my shoulder.

"Thorns can hurt you," I whispered.

"I know."

Her reply was quieter than a whisper and I could almost feel her heart pound. I put one arm around her, looked her in the eyes and saw her blush, so a part of my face, I couldn't even tell which one, touched her neck softly, not daring to look at her face to see the reaction. I felt lips on my neck and sticky wine on my cheek. "You'll never wash me away," she whispered.

"I won't."

Suddenly, I heard the sound of breaking glass that made me shudder – it was the empty bottle of wine.

"Is that your thing?" I asked. Lily laughed.

"Don't apologise," I said.

-

The night before she left, I heard a knock on my door.
"Lily."

"Rose."

She looked me in the eyes, incapable of saying anything. I locked the door behind us and kissed her in our very own Garden of Eden.

-

The morning she left, all I had left to give her was a rose. I had picked a rose from my own garden, knowing that once it's picked, it would die sooner or later. I gave it to her without saying anything and she started crying. I knew what she was thinking. She knew what I was thinking. And I knew she knew I knew.

It had been an amazing summer. But now it was over. I needed to go back to university in less than a week and before I did that, I needed to help my parents clean up the place – and then wait until next spring.

Our summer had been wonderful. And I knew there would never be anyone who would change my summer in unexpected ways like these. Not anymore. This had been *our* summer, would always be ours.

What we had – nobody else ever will. At least not with me.

So many words were left unspoken, but we didn't say them, because we didn't need to. Now I knew she didn't hate it when I knew things.

-

… because lilies bloom from early summer to fall. The frost during winter can be fatal for lilies. If they freeze to death, they die, never to come back again.

-

Our summer was wonderful, but now winter is over and I still think about you.

But at least I remember all of this.

<u>by</u>

"Bye." And that was it.

As the door of the train closed on my last time in London and I saw her eyes that seemed to express something I didn't understand back then, as I saw the train move no matter how hard I was trying to hold it back with my thoughts and somehow convince it to just stay, I realised that there are some things that I simply have no control over. Back then I didn't know that I was never coming back and that I wasn't going to see the lights of the city or the lights of her eyes ever again.

"Our last goodbye." Maybe she whispered these words after the doors had closed, maybe she didn't.

As the train started moving, the lights simply faded away, were taken away and consumed by the speed of the train.

This city and this soul that had felt like home to me and that had shaped me in ways I could never describe with words were left behind and maybe a small part of me (that wasn't too tired to do or think anything at all) knew. Maybe there had been something… a hint, a look, a sentence, an emotion.

And maybe I could have realised it sooner, but I loved to believe that the lights I was leaving behind were only temporarily gone and that with the help of money and trains and planes I had the power to bring them back at any time; I used to believe that I could even skip work, call in sick or pretend to have an important appointment: I could skip my important appointments just to go back to London and see the lights any time I wanted. In fact, I believed that I could simply move to London so all the lights of the city would forever be mine.

I used to believe in my own power. I used to believe in controlling everything.

But the train kept rolling.

At this moment, I didn't jump out of the moving train, but if I had thought about it at this very minute, if I had realised what was going on, I would probably have done it, just to see another light, to embrace it, to keep it and to consume it until we would have become one and until there would have been nothing left of me.

And the lights became darker. Is there such a thing as a black light? A blackness that is not entirely black, but a blackness that shines, that radiates its darkness... because that was how it felt as I approached my "home" which didn't feel like one. I was taken by this entity of radiating darkness of which I was not even entirely sure whether it existed or not.

Soon, she was gone from my life. The lights had gone out. At this point, I was sure I was never going to return. Why would I? I had no reason.

As soon as she uttered the words, as soon as she left me, I realised what I had felt at the train station. What I had seen in her eyes hadn't been her own lights.

Her eyes had been dark the entire day, not filled with any emotions, not telling me anything, as if she had been blind or absent or dead, because she had made a definite and final decision that I didn't have access to or any kind of influence on. What I had seen in her eyes that day, what I had seen in her eyes on the train station were not the lights in her eyes.

We had lost our connection.

I had only seen a deceitful reflection of one of the many lights of this beautiful city, London.

breaking my heart

I am invisible, but what if I wrote about myself for once?

Buckle your seatbelts, I am in control now. Why? Because I say so. This is my book and I can write whatever I want.

Imagine a whip. I know you just did. See? I am in control.

Let me tell you a secret.

I pretend to know, I pretend to know more than all of you, but in reality, all I do is lie and tell the truth at the same time.

I hide in the shadows to observe you: you never asked for a story about yourself, but here it is, without your consent. Can you find yourself?

I can turn you into a villain, into my friend, into my mother, my father, my boyfriend, my girlfriend or I can just write about the uncensored you and then pretend that I'm writing about someone I invented.

I write about myself. I write about the things that I see, the things I care about.

I write about you. I want you to understand, I want you to feel what I'm trying to make you feel even if you usually don't feel this at all.

My poems don't even rhyme. I'm so glad someone pointed it out – I didn't know. I wrote them when I was drunk. Or maybe I lied?

Are the words that you are reading right now fiction? The lines between the real world and this one are really blurry.

Do I ever tell you the truth?

pepper,
milk,
sugar and tea
and two spoons of something
I can't remember.

If I told you this was a poem, you'd believe it. Is it a poem or did I copy and paste my shopping list?

What is a poem? Is it a poem as soon as it rhymes? Is it a poem

as soon
as I break it up
into
paragraphs?

Do you refuse to call this a poem because it doesn't rhyme?

This is a poem because I say so. Everything I write turns into a poem as soon as I say so.

But can I ever not write about myself? Who am I writing about if it isn't myself?

If I say so, then I can. Remember: I'm in control. I turn stories into lies and I hide a truth somewhere. Can you find it?

I write about you and you and you and you breaking my heart. But the "I" in "my" is not even me. When I write "I", the "I" is just a perspective. Who am I?

Let's play hide and seek: I'm going to hide between my own lines, except you'll never find me. This is a book. Go on, try to grab the page by the throat and scream out all the questions you have.

Maybe you should ask yourself these questions. If you want to scream out questions, scream them out in front of the mirror. The mirror isn't going to answer. But that's you in the mirror, isn't it? Don't worry: The mirrors in the real world always show you your own reflection.

This book is about *you* for a reason.

Maybe there is white ink on the pages that tells you the truth. How would you know? Find it out if you can.

I'll meet you in the shadows. We'll try to find the white ink together or maybe you'll be one of the villains who inspire my art.

Catch me if you can and break my heart.

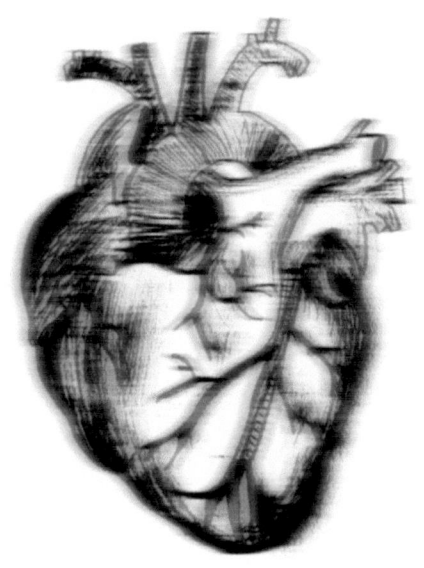

POETRY

Warped, distorted, blurry faces
of a raven and a calf,
liquidating, melting, pouring
down into a dirty shaft.
We keep running. We keep running.

Peaky sheep stand in dark corners
asking if we need their aid.
Stepping on them to climb higher
and into the night we fade.
We keep running. We keep running.

Narrow alleys in the darkness
lead us on eternal paths,
we run in circles, we don't know-
lost between our fear and wrath,
we keep running. We keep running.

The raven, calf and sheep are back,
suddenly, they look like elves
and rising to the sky they say:
"You are running from yourselves."
We keep running. We keep running.

it's been a month
and then a year
(and writing it down makes it easier to believe)
now you are gone
and I'm still here

and I stand here
I built a grave
(here lies our love, our passion, my life)
to bury
everything you gave

(no grave is bittersweet enough
dark and bitter enough
like your favourite chocolate
like my room at noon
I remember
you used to be
so afraid
of losing me to the dark
am I supposed to bring flowers now
the ones that I hated and tried to forget
I used to bring you roses
I remember
no
forgetting, burying, leaving behind
not remembering
I was so afraid
of losing you in the light
in plain sight
but I did
I remember
bittersweet
lips so sweet
they tasted of honey and peaches

no
forgetting
I need to forget
I'm here to bury you, I'm sorry
I need to forget
no grave is bittersweet enough
I need to forget
no grave is bittersweet enough
to capture   )

There are galaxies inside you,
but do they liberate
or do they fight you?

Painting your face,
painting your eyes,
covering you
in my own lies.

Painting your soul
in blue and white,
your heart:
surrounded by the light.

Adding glitter
on your body
to fool myself
and everybody.

And now this painting
full of lies
attracts the butterflies.
They die.

Hello raven in my dream,
why don't you fly away?
Eating carrion in my room
and wanting me to stay?

My dear raven, what is wrong,
why don't you fly outside,
why do you just stare at me?
The window's open wide.

Sit on flowers, not on walls,
this is no place for you.
Rotten flesh makes me feel sick,
but still binds me to you.

We just sit there in a trance
and I can't help but stare
hypnotized and paralysed
as you land on my chair.

You are just one step away,
and the allure of nightfall
is what kills me, leaving blood
dripping from my bedroom wall.

Tell me, London, city of dreams,
are your lights as far as it seems?
Are your parks my future,
is your light my light,
guiding me though the depth of the night?

Tell me, London, city of dreams,
will you sometimes hear my screams?
Will you hear my whispers,
will you see when it's dark
inside my soul and inside my heart?

Tell me, you, the person of my dreams,
is our future as far as it seems?
Are your tears my tears
and when will they dry,
when will London's darkness die?

We were never perfect,
but we were close to "good"
and our souls collided
like no others ever could.

But every single time
I look at lilac skies,
I think of cotton candy
and your cotton candy lies.

It's winter now. I'm freezing,
stored our memories in my shelf,
I gave away your jackets,
I need to save myself.

When I heard you lying,
I started waking up.
When I ate your sweet cotton candy,
you thought of breaking up.

I put my life in boxes
and store them on my desk
until I finish packing,
until there's nothing left.

I put my clothes in closets
and I inhale their smell.
Maybe "knowing who I am"
is something I can't spell.

Two keys, two different houses
that I both call my home.
But which one is the one
that I would call my own?

Where's my heart when I come "home",
where is my mind, where is my soul,
which house knows all my secrets
and all my darkest holes?

Who am I when I'm coming?
Am I a visitor?
Where do I go when leaving?
Am I returning home?

Have you seen the bright stars between the dim ones?
Been wanting to pick one for you like a flower. I'm
asking what kind of flowers you like. We see
ourselves in a mirror. "What kind of flower do I look
like?"

So I couldn't answer. How
often have I tried to answer this question,
how often have I failed? I know you want a bouquet of
stars.

We are stars.
Are we bright enough?

Have been asking ourselves so often
how we are
that we forgot to be
(happy in between).

I knew it was the last time
when the doors were closing,
inevitably closing,
and it felt like this road
that had become my home
would lead me back one last time
to somewhere far from home.
It felt so different this time
when we said our goodbyes,
I feel like you were thinking,
"Have a nice rest of your life."
I thought that you had found
something I couldn't give
and maybe you had found
a way that you could live.
I looked out of the window,
bit my lip to hide the pain,
'cause if you weren't happy,
it would be all in vain.
Where am I going now without you,
what's my new gravity,
how am I gonna find it:
another destiny?

Yeah
you should go through hell,
not taking, always giving.
But if it hurt:
Oh well,
at least that's living.

I'm a glass cube filled with water,
do not break me,
'cause the water will be pouring
till you fix me.

Guess you better freeze my water,
crash my glass down,
you can break it all you want now,
I won't feel it.

You can put the shattered pieces
back together,
but will I ever be the same
if you lost some?

Screams, a mass of guilty voices
and vibration fills the air,
sometimes I just come and listen
to those souls so scarred and bare.

Chaos of letters, words and phrases
losing sound and sense and shape
and escaping only partly
from this lord's almighty gates.

"Our king," one voice is screaming,
now there's two, now three, now four,
"Our king," they're coming closer,
knocking on the portal door.

I freeze to death, burn back to life,
madness in hell has just begun,
as I faint, I hear them saying,
"Our king Lucifer is gone."

The darkness takes me by surprise,
escaping souls scream and cry,
our eyes start burning as they meet
and two worlds collide and die.

Waiting for summer

just so winter ends

only to regret

not having seen spring.

You were just a character,
I was the author of this mess.
I tried to write us both tonight
by saying much, revealing less.

Distorted eyes and lips and ears,
the mind has no restrictions,
your voice, your words, your thoughts are real,
your empathy is fiction.

And as you read yourself in this
distorted picture of yourself
you are looking at cold mirrors
and all you see is someone else.

It's 3 am
and I know that I
need more from you
than being kept awake
until 6 am
just by my thoughts
about starry nights
by the lake.

False notes
and old pianos
and playing
without notes
run on repeat
without a pause,
drift away, then come back
like the red and yellow boats.

Summers without you,
dreaming and swimming,
playing pianos
alone
like the bittersweet taste
of the clair de lune-
it haunts me.
I want (you) to be home.

Blood
runs through my veins,
makes its way through my system
to keep me alive.
My cheeks turn red,
the blood stays for a while
because they told me
that I have to lie -
I see children,
I am a child,
I see people and bodies
that look just like mine.
They say and they talk and they tell
what happens between bedsheets at night,
who has done what
and who's done it right
how it has to be done and how often,
who has to man up or to soften.
But suddenly
silence is golden
when a thousand silver knifes
stab me, kill me
and eat me alive
inside my belly,
cut me in half -
so my blood leaves my body
and colours my bedsheets -
they said we can not talk about this.
Am I ruining the picture?
Aren't we all bleeding?
Inside and out, her body and his?

Devils slit his wrists and they
pumped poison through his veins
to put him back together
with stitches and with chains.

Black and dirty poison
is running through his veins.
Hurt, tied up, distorted,
he lies there in his chains.

When he was crying rainbows,
the devils thought there had been rain
and when he drowns in love,
they start to operate his brain.

They turned him to a robot
and broke him from within.
When he is bleeding rainbows,
they paint black on his skin.

When he's crying rainbows,
He's stuffed with ash and coal
they put salt in his wound
to fill the empty hole.

Mirror, mirror on the wall,
the devils ask, "What do you see?"
He says, "I see the devil.
He's standing next to me."

All those shattered parts of him
on every rainy day,
on nights that hide his colours
still live - what can I say?

They broke him into pieces
and they spat on his heart.
Thank you for inspiring
the villains in my art.

They open their mouths
and speak about violence,
our youth
will never be silenced.

Your youth is dead,
their vocal cords cut,
their minds are poisoned,
their eyes are shut.

Our women are strong,
the ones who bleed and who don't,
the ones who'll give birth
and the ones that won't.

Your women: dependant,
will-less and oppressed,
insulted and beaten
for the way they are dressed.

We hear and we think and act
with reason and heart.
We unite people
you're keeping apart.

Two men holding guns
is what makes them male,
but two men holding hands
is what brings them to jail?

A voice for the youth
to cure the wound that ails
and less nuclear weapons
for cishet, white, old males.

Can you find yourself?
(truth)
Can you find the truth between the li(n)es?
(lie)
Find it out if you can.

I'm calm in spring
'cause my demons can rest,
I'm resting
because my demons aren't
chasing a life,
they love being dead.
And I also love
when they are dead
and sometimes I think
where life actually happens
is inside a train,
not the flowers that bloom,
not the children with their happy feet,
just waiting.
The man over there;
eating, then reading,
waiting to get to his wife.
Not only is he waiting,
not only is he reading,
he's living his life,
living a lie?
The woman over there;
writing
a letter to the one that she loves.
She's living life deeply,
silently weeping
and waiting for the one that she loves.
But is someone waiting
in their homes
where the flowers of spring
do not bloom?

(You're not real.)
You hide in neon colours.
Champagne and vodka
and pills are dancing
to your favourite song.
(You're not here.)
Blurry drinks and people
and words that they say
that sound like something else,
like something they wouldn't.
(You're in a dream.)
You wonder if you could write poems now,
you have so much to say, so much to share,
you wish you could read out your poems,
you need to-
(use the bathroom or wake up.)

Thirteen pictures
in a frame,
thirteen faces,
thirteen names.

Thirteen smiles
carved in stone
looking at me
from their throne.

Thirteen lies
on the wall,
they will never
ever fall.

The first time they saw the galaxies in each other
felt like swimming for the first time with her mother.
"Mummy, it's cold!" – shaking feet, heavy breath.
The child knows that drowning would be its death.
"Don't be scared, my child, it's just water!"
she says and holds the hand of her daughter.
Maybe drowning isn't the end.
You're just surrounded by something you can't
comprehend.
You're so covered in it, so full you could burst,
but you need the water to allay your thirst.
Some galaxies meet, turn into one and unite,
they drown together, far away from the light,
far away from the mother's hand,
deeper than anyone could understand.

Hate is your anchor,
but seas are too deep.
You see the surface,
but don't know what's beneath.
Welcome to a world
that you'll never see.
You think of a puddle,
but this is a sea.

cities burn
burn my eyes out
so I can't see
what's left of human life
we are dying
dyeing hair
it looks so good
just don't look
we are crying
this movie is good
close the curtains
don't look at the flames
we are buying
clothes and games
citics burn
down in flames

Speak up.
Think.
Read the white ink.
Don't let them in.
Don't let them win.
That's not a sin.
I haven't read the book,
I'm sorry.
But don't you interpret
every story?
Think.
There is no white ink.
Forgive the big guy,
he's not a writer.
He sometimes wishes
his angels' halos were brighter.
If you don't see,
it's not your fault.
Think.
Even sugar looks like salt.

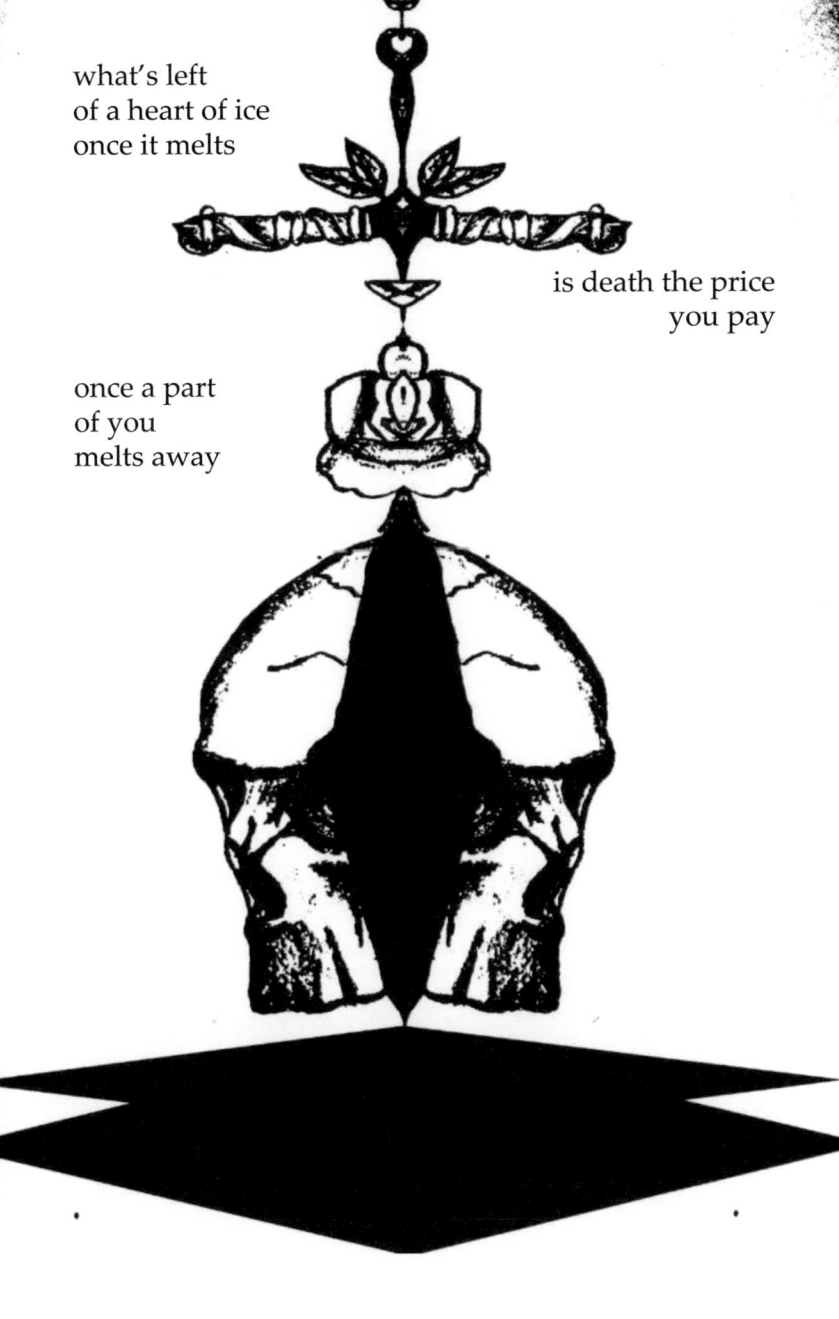

what's left
of a heart of ice
once it melts

is death the price
you pay

once a part
of you
melts away

Driving backwards
means you're moving.
Crashing
means that you're alive.
Crashing
means you're moving.
Driving backwards?
You'll arrive.

"Don't be mad, please.
I know I didn't reply.
You didn't hurt me.
I just needed time to think.
I hope you don't think
their messages are more important.
I don't know if you'll stay
if I ask you to.
I'm gonna say it:
they are less important.
No one is more
important than you."

- toxic conversation

Hello, doctor.
Good to see you, too.
But how are *you*?
(Confusion.
Confused thoughts about infusions.)
That's okay.
It can wait.
Did you eat?
Don't you want to
take a seat?
(Question.
Confused thoughts about ingestion.)
Because I want to know.
You look tired.
You should go home.
You're the only one who cures
people's bodies,
but not your own.

Is her dress
"too provoking"?
I understand.
So is your nose.
Now that it's bleeding,
how do you feel?
I'm so sorry.
Let me apologise
with a rose.

I called her by my name
when I realised
blue was the warmest colour.
I watched Watson and Holmes
being handcuffed
to each other.
I've seen rainbow characters die,
I've seen Elio cry
by the fireplace.
Holmes said
Sherlock was actually a girl's name
and maybe blue is the warmest colour
because that's how they felt
without one another.
They knew.
I watch all of this too
when I feel blue
every now and then.
It helps me
to feel warm again.

(deep poem)
a tablespoon of sugar
a little piece of something
I think it was cake?
just a few eggs
salad for my sister
avocado and a lemon
milk
(this is my grocery list)

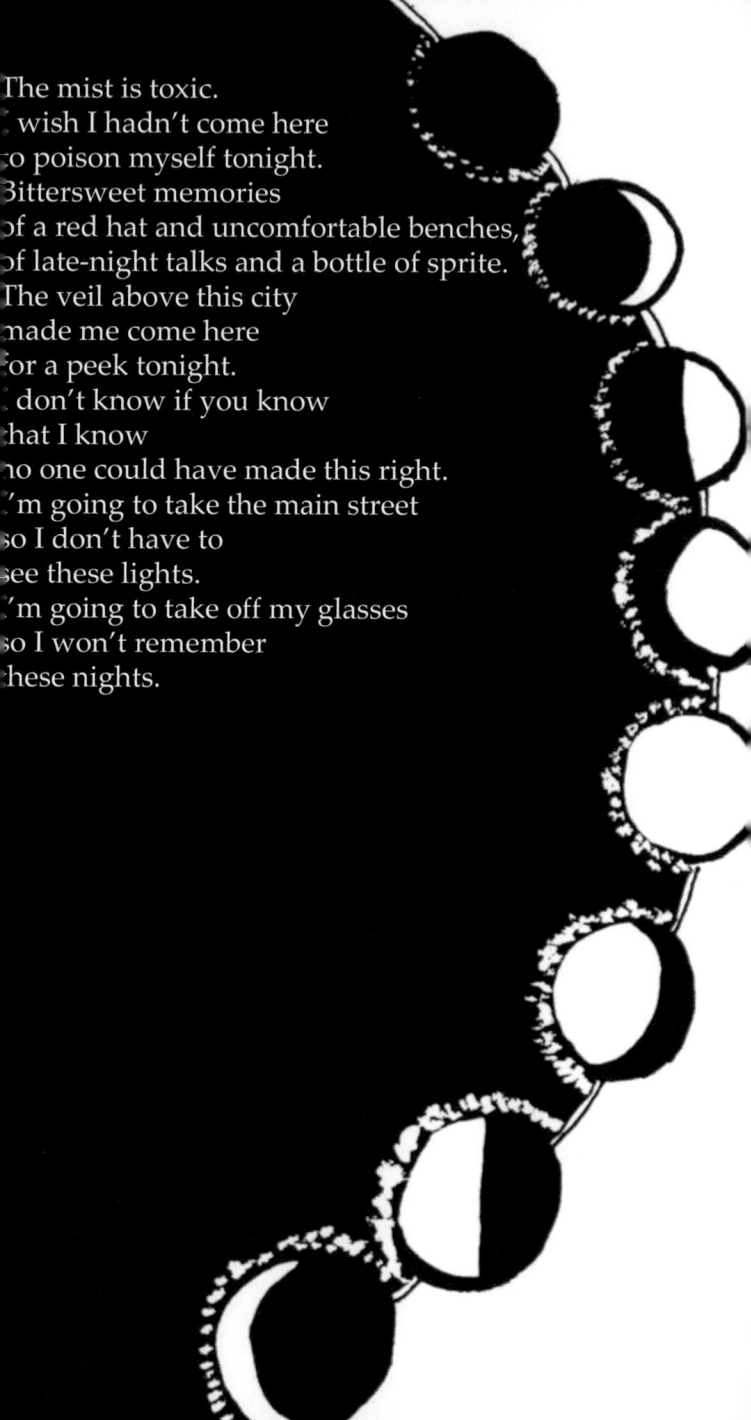

The mist is toxic.
I wish I hadn't come here
to poison myself tonight.
Bittersweet memories
of a red hat and uncomfortable benches,
of late-night talks and a bottle of sprite.
The veil above this city
made me come here
for a peek tonight.
I don't know if you know
that I know
no one could have made this right.
I'm going to take the main street
so I don't have to
see these lights.
I'm going to take off my glasses
so I won't remember
these nights.

There was no reason for her
not to be there
and no reason for me
to check the list.
So I decided to go
for a walk
with the devil
and smiled like the first time we kissed.

"I'd really love to come, but-
you know, linguistics.
And I haven't started studying
for statistics."
You liar.
Linguistics was three semester ago.
Why don't you explain
why you don't wanna go?
"You're such a poor thing.
First, there was the death of your cat
three times in a row
and now you have to put up with that!"
Did she believe it?
I feel like she did.
She never notices
when I talk shit.
"I'll be there next time,
I bet it'll be fun!
Anyway, text me!
I gotta run!"

"Hey, what's up!
Let's meet up again!"

"I'm sorry,
I have an appointment at ten."

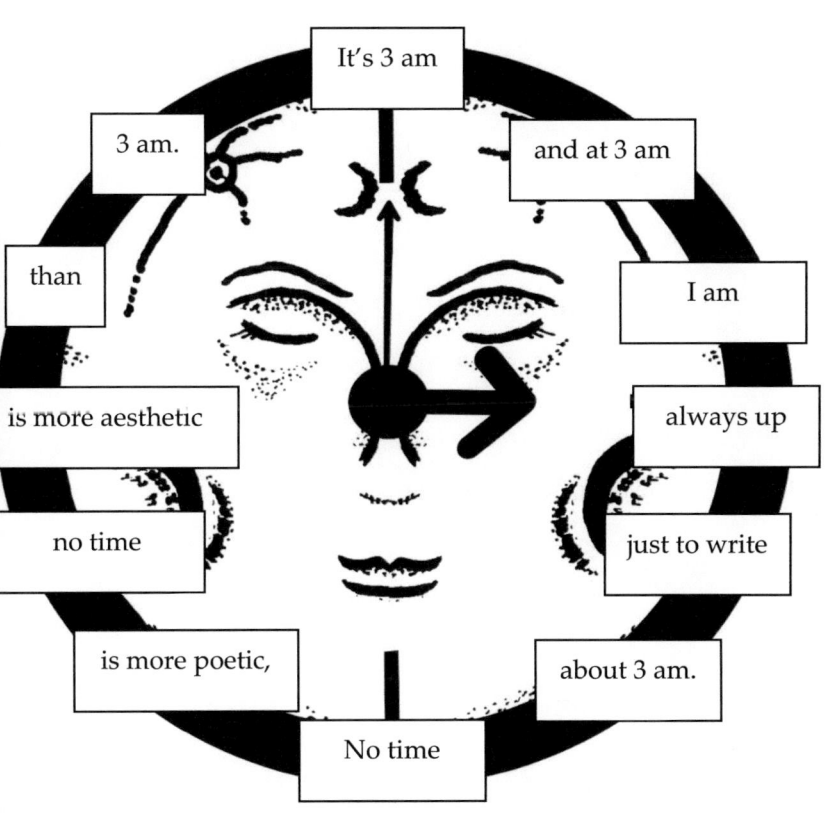

It's 3 am

3 am.

and at 3 am

than

I am

is more aesthetic

always up

no time

just to write

is more poetic,

about 3 am.

No time

97

I swear to you
that trees have eyes
that discover
all your lies
pupils
eyelids
don't you see
you can't trust
your eyes
your pupils
when you see
pupils and eyelids
in the darkness?
I swear
the forest talks
about you
when you take your walks
susurration
in an empty forest
sounds
sounds like a man
without a voice
desperate attempt
trying to make
a noise
sister, listen, whispers
come come come
don't trust the whispers
behind your back
or whisper back?
I swear
their roots are feet
and I can hear
their hearts that beat
pulsation

me?
someone?
behind me?
turn around quickly
beat beat
beat beat
is someone behind me?
can I trust my heart
when I hear a heart beat?

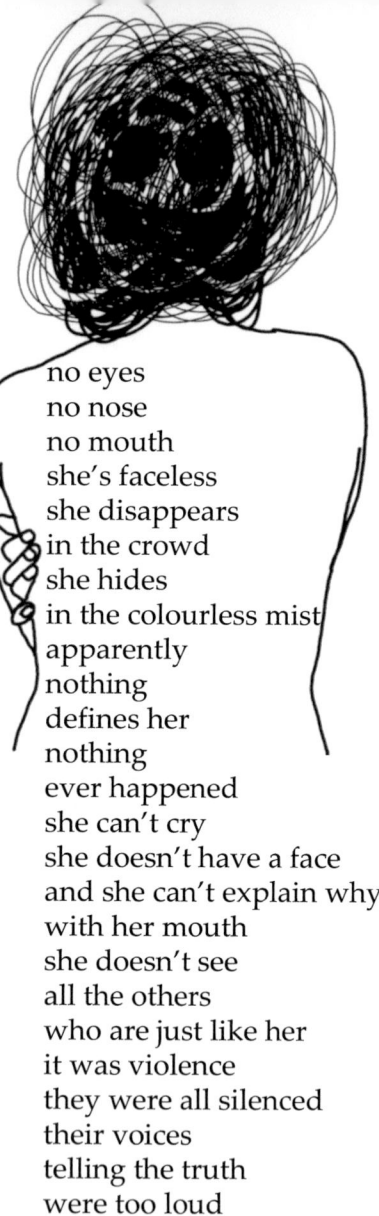

no eyes
no nose
no mouth
she's faceless
she disappears
in the crowd
she hides
in the colourless mist
apparently
nothing
defines her
nothing
ever happened
she can't cry
she doesn't have a face
and she can't explain why
with her mouth
she doesn't see
all the others
who are just like her
it was violence
they were all silenced
their voices
telling the truth
were too loud
now they have
no eyes

no nose
no mouth
no one can see
no one can listen
no one can shout
they hide
in the crowd

They took off
their skin,
threw it on the floor.
They were both bleeding,
but they wanted more.
They ripped out their eyes,
they hadn't seen much.
I could write porn
about the way
their hearts touched.

End credits:
cast:
the past
that shaped me,
ghosts that
escaped me,
directed by
crackheads
on amphetamines and
sleeping pills
on toxic liquids
with a toxic mind
where the real and the fake
are undefined,
produced by
the world in black and white
between six in the morning
and three at night,
music by
my black guitar,
I play it while
I smoke my cigar,
I wish I could see it unfiltered,
I want to rip out
my eyeballs with the black tattoo
just to see,
editor: me.

Thank you for reading this book.
Thank you for supporting my weird art.
You made my childhood wish come true.

Is there anything you want to tell me?
Feel free to contact me via ohnevermind@gmx.net !